Found God by Accident

A Self-Help Journey
Turned Great & Terrible Encounter

A True Story

Jordon J. Schultz

Found God by Accident: A Self-help Journey Turned Great & Terrible Encounter - A True Story

By Jordon Schultz

Copyright © 2022 by Jordon Schultz

Unless otherwise noted, all scripture quotations taken from The Amplified Bible, Copyright © 1954, 1958, 1962, 1964, 1965, 1987, 2015 by The Lockman Foundation. All rights reserved. Used by permission.

No part of this book may be reproduced or transmitted in any form or by any means, electronic or mechanical, including photocopying, recording, or by any information storage and retrieval system–except for brief quotations, without written permission from the author.

All rights reserved.

Printed in the United States of America

Cover & Layout Design by Dana Bowen

This Book Is Dedicated To:

Meu Amor (My Love),

Honestly, I questioned how a wife is considered favor from the Lord. Through seasons of feast and famine, you continue to show me this truth in God's word.

Thank you for showing me when I am wrong and being gracious when I take my medicine; for being patient with me when I am not gracious toward you; for being a great mother; and for being a beautiful woman of God by actively displaying your love for me.

You often say love is a decision and not a feeling. Thank you for not quitting on me.

Te Amo,

Jordon

Ecclesiastes 4:9-12

Table of Contents

Deep Reflection	8
Childhood to Adulting	17
The Run-In with Authority	27
Not Going to Church	32
The Battle Begins	37
All Hope Lost	43
Faith	50
Hope	60
Love	70
Unconditional Love of God	78
Known by God	84
Afterword	91
Acknowledgments	94

Introduction

Between the ropes in a fight I never knew existed, I taunted life. Raised was my right hand after I stacked some wins, and my left after my first product invention went viral. Sure, I took a few jabs here and there, but my jaw had become seasoned over the years. Then I learned life is a southpaw; I never saw the haymaker coming.

Dazed and confused, I slowly examined myself to discover how I never saw this coming. I ripped off the band-aids that covered my problems, and as I tended my wounds, I found God by complete accident.

Unfortunately, during the 10-count, life took a cheap shot and kicked me down. No disqualification. No redo. And no cutman until the round was over. I had to get up; I had no choice.

Somehow, I stumbled to the corner where God fixed me up. The pain was heart-wrenching as He pressed the eye iron to my pride, jammed gauze pads deep into my emotional cuts, and put ice packs on my addictions. He then liberally applied the petroleum jelly and threw me back into the fight. Gradually, miracle after miracle took place as I fought back with every ounce of strength that remained.

This is my story of redemption from a God Whom I thought was dead.

Deep Reflection

January 3rd, 2019

As I pondered how my life went from the top of the world with my first product invention that went viral to rock bottom and in my mother's basement, I knew it was time to be brutally honest with myself. Truth be told, my life was much worse than fresh out of a meaningful relationship and back to the basement life again at twenty-nine years old. I had a controlled but uncontrolled addiction to snorting Adderall, a disgusting pornography habit, a fearless addiction to nicotine and smoking marijuana, and so much more. My addictions were so bad that my addictions had addictions.

I was a master at hiding my true self, and these surface stains were just the beginning of the terror I felt if, one day, the real Jordon was ever exposed. I was beyond lost in life, afraid to be an outcast, and I was alone. I was desperate to get to the bottom of my pain and conflicts, so I turned the camera of life on myself and tried to capture every little thought, fear, insecurity, and weakness with the resolve to fix everything. No stone was left unturned.

As I prepared for my final semester at the Wisconsin School of Business, I knew it was important to straighten myself before I took on the workload of a top business school in the country. My typical routine consisted of snorting a 10mg Adderall and swallowing another in the morning, packing my mouth full of Grizzly Wintergreen Pouches throughout the day, working on my shot glass invention, and smoking marijuana when I needed a quick break.

My baby-step self-improvement journey started with nicotine because it was the habit I was most ashamed of. Like many others, my past attempts to quit had failed, so I turned to Chantix for my final quest to conquer this beast. Aware of the potential side effects, I knew being in the correct state of mind was extremely important. After I held onto the medication for a couple of weeks, I was ready to get started.

January 8th, 2019

The next step involved help from others. I turned to other entrepreneurs in a Facebook group who recommended the book Think and Grow Rich by Napoleon Hill. Before downloading the book on Spotify, I made a deep vow and fully sold out to just do what the guy told me to do. The world humbled me, and I was not going to let the world win again.

While I cleaned out the old junk in my room and listened to this book, Napoleon Hill prescribed a daily routine. I knew, without a doubt, I needed to write this down. Here is the list of items of the routine:

- One minute of laughter

- Expression of gratitude for wins and losses

- Give thanks for blessings expected to receive that day

- Can do and start action

- All negative actions and thoughts turned into positive action

- Always learning and on alert for education

- Express gratitude two times per day for control over your own mind and ask for guidance

- Compliment good qualities in people

- All criticism for oneself is learning and analysis

- Do not accept anything that you do not desire

- Find your major purpose in life

   I started that very night. As I forced myself to laugh, this one minute felt like waiting for the day after forever. However, the determination I had was more than enough to get past the thoughts of how crazy this might look if someone saw me laughing for no reason with my phone timer in hand.

January 16th, 2019

Full dedication to this list took time, but I slowly discovered I had taken the little things in life for granted. I had a warm place to stay, food to eat, a reliable car, and a supportive family. This immediate meditation on thankfulness shocked me as I discovered this poor attitude existed. At that moment, I was even slightly thankful to be in this vulnerable state and how everything in my life had just crumbled.

As shocking as this lack of thankfulness was, I reflected more on understanding what it meant to express gratitude for control over your mind and ask for guidance (Item 7). With full sincerity, I began to ask myself what it meant to control my mind and who in the world I asked for guidance from. Little did I know, but I was about to find out.

January 17th, 2019

The self-improvement chase was in full swing, and a huge breakthrough finally occurred. Lost in my thoughts while driving, I pondered about controlling my thoughts again. As I ventured to truly understand the meaning, I quickly realized I was thinking about some random topic that had nothing to do with controlling my thoughts. Upon this realization, my mind snapped back to the initial topic at hand, and then it hit me. I just fought off the lack of focus as I tried to understand what controlling my mind meant and wrestled my mind back to attention.

I went ballistic as I knew I had just discovered something truly incredible. I had no idea that anyone could actually capture and control their mind and thoughts! As a believer in how powerful a human mind can be, I was hyped and curious about what I could accomplish with this new skill I had found. Eager to press on, the day ended with the routine checklist and a renewed hope for tomorrow.

January 18th, 2019

Hair still wet from a morning shower, list in hand, and a new sense of energy, I was on my knees this time. After the awkward laugh, my mind was now stuck on asking for guidance. With a confused look on my face, I said aloud, "Who am I asking for guidance from?" I immediately scoffed as I thought about the churches and the God they preach about. The God they talk about is not real because if that God was real, then why have I witnessed such terrible people come from those places?

With these thoughts, feelings, and the desire to keep moving forward, I turned to the next best thing - horoscopes and astrology. I quickly found a horoscope App and was impressed at its deadly accuracy. I was so impressed that I went from 0 to 100 and consumed as much information as fast as I could. In less than two days, I thought I had just discovered another truly incredible thing!

That afternoon, strange and supernatural things started to happen. Numbers and letters popped off the street signs as if I were watching a 3D movie. Experienced from mind-bending trips on psychedelic mushrooms, acid, and salvia, I knew this was completely different. Something was trying to communicate with me. Now in detective mode, I found an astrology number key and simply went along with what was happening. Knowing how crazy this would sound, I kept all of this to myself and continued down this adventure which became more and more interesting by the day.

January 19th, 2019

The daily routine was still going strong, and the supernatural craziness continued. At one point, a number jumped out to me from a street sign correlated to "Jesus" from the astrology key. Completely turned off from God, Jesus, and the fake religion I grew up with, this moment did not register with me. It was as if it had never happened.

The horoscope informed me I would have a run-in with authority on Tuesday. I immediately mocked this horoscope stuff, but I knew this was the ultimate test to see if this horoscope nonsense was legit. So, it was settled. Like Kevin McCallister in Home Alone, I was going to do everything in my power to ensure this run-in with authority would not take me down.

January 22nd, 2019

Confident I was about to discredit astrology and horoscopes, the run-in with authority day arrived. Before I headed off to my second day of spring semester classes, I did the usual Adderall routine and made the extra effort with my mother and stepfather to make sure they were not the source of this run-in. My marijuana and one-hitter stash no longer had their usual hiding spot as I completed a top-to-bottom cleaning of my car that guaranteed to keep me out of trouble with the police.

At home early from a light day of class, sitting on the couch and thinking about all of this out-of-my-mind nonsense, I was not able to get past the fact that I knew something was happening, but I had no deep conviction yet. Not a single event could prove to someone I was not crazy.

Moments later, I set my phone down after typing out a response to a Facebook post and turned my head slightly to the left. I noticed this unusual darkness in the room, but it was not due to the lack of lighting. Immediately, this darkness cut across my entire field of vision as if I had removed a pair of sunglasses, but this darkness moved from left to right. The contrast between the trailing edge of this darkness and the light was so distinct. I instantly jumped to my feet with deep conviction and said, "Now I know something is going on."

With zero understanding of this visual experience, 9 pm rolled around, and it was time to wrap up the day. I proudly laughed because I officially discredited this horoscope garbage, so I completed the routine list and was ready for bed. Unfortunately, I was not the one with the last laugh because this run-in with authority was just minutes away.

Childhood to Adulting

I was raised in a broken family, and I have no memories of my parents as a married couple. I do not understand why, but my mother left her five kids, and it was my father's responsibility to make things work. She did return after her two-year hiatus when I was in the second grade, but I still remember the tears when I tried to use our rotary phone while my sister told me there was no way to talk to my mommy. The damage was done.

My older siblings said they never felt as if our mother was gone for long periods, but my memories tell a different story. One Mother's Day, my first-grade teacher even suggested gifting my aunt along with my mother, a person I consider a mother figure in my life and is responsible for many great qualities I have today. The point is, I am thankful my father had a great support system around him, and he still credits the help from others for getting through this period in our lives.

I am not trying to communicate that I had the worst childhood. In fact, there are more positive memories than there are bad memories. My favorite memories are the road trips to a family cabin in Northern Wisconsin. These road trips were jam sessions with Styx, Queen, Journey, and Foreigner. We rocked out while we pretended to be the band playing the songs. In the old conversion van with those sweet captain chairs that spun around, my sister was the lead singer, two boys in the middle seats as guitar and bass players, and a drummer in the back. There was always a fight about who was the odd man out in the back who did not have a dedicated position in the band.

Things got sketchy, however, when my dad met another woman when I was in the fourth grade. My dad, who found someone to love us kids as her own, sparked something evil inside of our mother that caused a cascade of lingering effects that are evident even today. She created half-truths and lies with the intent to cause hatred and division toward our dad. It was as if our mom tried to brainwash us with the ultimate goal to convince us to live with her and abandon our dad. I believe the main objective was to create as much pain for our dad as possible.

One by one and for years, psychological warfare certainly took its toll. This did not work on my sister, my two older brothers were sucked in, I was a half-casualty, and my youngest brother made it through. During my sophomore year in high school, it was my turn to be the subject of abuse to bring revenge on our dad. There are many examples to share, but this is the one that killed me in this battle.

I was a kid in high school who had a fear of missing out. Our dad had rules to follow, and our mom was always working. Mom always working meant no rules, so I was able to do whatever I wanted and appease this fear of missing out. I was persuaded to abandon my dad and stay full-time with my mom. In hindsight, the destruction this caused was evident only years later as I reflected on the behaviors and habits I developed after these events occurred.

Living out of a suitcase and going back and forth between homes every week was one of my least favorite things to experience in my childhood and played into my decision to abandon my dad. Even though this psychological warfare was in full swing, my dad and stepmom never gave up when it came to their involvement and participation in my life. They showed up to nearly every soccer game, baseball game, and every other major event in my life. The number of times my mom showed up to sporting events could be counted on one hand.

I am baffled by the grit my dad and stepmom showed, as they never gave up during this battle. My dad did not have a choice but to imagine four young boys who loved sports and WCW wrestling. Our stepmom broke up more than her fair share of beatdowns, body slams, and Stone Cold Stunners. She even claims she was on the receiving end of a haymaker delivered by yours truly. For whatever reason, she stuck with us, and I still get tears when I think about the amount of trash she put up with. She has been the most incredible stepmother anyone could have asked for and a great example of love that never quits.

High School

I loved to learn, so I was diligent in my schooling and maintained top grades. After seeing my sister's graduation, I set a goal in the sixth grade to make it on the stage for my high school graduation. I accomplished this goal and graduated in the top 10% of my high school class.

However, since I was always focused on getting good grades, I was a loner at school from the time I set this goal until my freshman year. That changed during my sophomore year when I found a group of kids who accepted me. This is when the fear of missing out kicked in, and my mom saw her opportunity to strike. For the longest time, I participated in the shenanigans, but I never did anything crazy like drink alcohol, smoke pot, or smash mailboxes. But in truth, we were troublemakers to the extreme!

Unfortunately, it did not take long before I eventually caved in and became this wild child like my friends. The joke was always about how they corrupted me. One thing led to another; before anyone had a clue, we all had addiction problems. From drinking parties to marijuana to OxyContin-the fall was hard and fast for most of us.

United States Air Force

Toward the end of high school, I wanted to go to college, but I knew I had to grow up first. If I had gone to college, I was certain I would have partied my way to failure. So, I joined the Air Force instead, and this decision was truly one of the best decisions I have made. I was now aware of the warfare between my parents, so the relationship with my dad was quickly restored. In fact, my dad and stepmom were the only ones there to send me off to boot camp.

For two years, I had dreamt and planned out my experience in the Air Force. To be honest, everything went exactly to plan. I graduated top in my Aircrew Flight Equipment training class, was stationed in Germany for two years, traveled all over Europe, and was even awarded two F16 backseat incentive flights for top performance. The military helped me mature, but I was still a wild child and did many things that would have gotten me kicked out in a heartbeat. This is not an excuse, but I am extremely thankful I never got caught. I am not afraid of this history, but if I could go back, there is a laundry list of things I would change.

Wisconsin School of Business–University of Wisconsin-Madison

After four years in the military, I decided to separate and attend engineering school at the Milwaukee School of Engineering in Milwaukee, Wisconsin. Again, I did well academically, but the transition back to civilian life was more difficult than I thought. I felt lost and eventually decided to leave school to find myself. I did some odds-and-ends jobs to learn and add new skills to my developing skill set. This was when I discovered I had a major interest in Business.

I started my business schooling at the Wisconsin School of Business, which has been my dream since high school. As I moved through my classes, I decided to take the fearful jump to launch this shot glass product I had invented five years prior. I was terrified but more afraid of not knowing what would happen. So, I took the leap, and as I learned something new in school, I applied the concepts to my product invention almost immediately. To be clear, I had to learn most of the knowledge and skills on my own, but business school certainly helped in the area of accounting.

From manufacturing in China to the entire e-commerce website, I set up the entire supply chain myself without any experience. After my friends and I got drunk and produced the marketing video, I posted it on YouTube. Within a week, a media company with 30 million followers on Facebook shared the video. Then BOOM–it went viral, and I was in disbelief. The fears I had all of those years were lies, and I was proud of myself for the courage to jump. I laugh about this now, but the website crashed during the viral explosion. However, orders from all over the world rushed in.

Attention Deficit Hyperactivity Disorder

I was diagnosed with ADHD when I was twenty-eight years old. This condition or superpower, when managed properly, helped me excel in many ways. I love the metaphor one doctor gave me: an ADHD brain is like a Ferrari without brakes. The challenge for me, and still is at times, is tuning the brakes.

I played around with Adderall in high school but never had a problem with it. I noticed something was off when I discovered my testing anxiety at the Wisconsin School of Business. I was never challenged at that level before, so when I recognized I was constantly reading and rereading exam questions, it hit me that something was wrong. Then I looked back and found multiple different scenarios that began to make sense.

For example, I would look directly into the eyes of people as they spoke to me, but I would often not hear what they said. I literally thought I was losing my hearing when I constantly asked people to repeat things.

It sounds silly, especially as I considered how I would pass the Air Force hearing tests with flying colors.

I also never had an explanation as to why I would often miss highway exits after I coached myself not to miss them. Or the anxiety that crippled me when I could not remember if I locked the house door or not. It all made sense - there were disconnects in my working memory!

Taking medication for ADHD is not the simple fix others think it is. Getting to where I am today required more work than I ever imagined. Is Adderall used and abused in college as a performance enhancer? I am sure it is. But to those who have this one-sided viewpoint, put yourself in someone's shoes for a moment.

Do you know what it is like to read a paragraph and then have to read it again because you do not remember a single thing you just read? Do you know the frustration of trying to find the things you misplaced? Do you understand the toll on relationships with these types of short-term memory failures? I will never forget the time when an old girlfriend told me her beloved grandfather had passed away, and I completely forgot about it. The point here is to please take caution the next time you judge in this arena.

The Run-In with Authority

The day is January 22, 2019, and this horoscope informed me I was about to have a run-in with authority. When the evening rolled around, I thought, for sure, I was free and clear. I was wrong.

Shortly after 9 pm, this voice inside my head that I believed to be my own thoughts told me to snort an Adderall and do some research on a certain topic. As a research junkie, I love to get lost in rabbit holes on the internet and soak up as much information as possible. After this voice told me to snort this Adderall, I verbally said aloud, "No, that is a STUPID idea. I would like to go to bed tonight." After about ten minutes of contemplation, I was hesitant but decided to follow this voice and explore something new.

Crushed, snorted, and ready to go, I felt like an idiot because it was so late in the day. I opened the horoscope App and navigated to the current time and day. What I read next instantly changed my life...

"WATCH OUT FOR DECEPTION"

My heart sank into my stomach as if I were caught red-handed, and this powerful presence filled the room. I dropped my phone, turned around, and was met by a dark, transparent silhouette of a person who was floor-to-ceiling tall. I collapsed to the floor and instantly knew at that moment that God was real.

On the floor and completely debilitated, words cannot describe how absolutely terrifying this moment was. I was before the Creator, and He judged me. As my life flashed before my eyes, the weight of every person I wronged, every terrible act I committed, and every disgusting character trait I had were on top of me. Deep down, I felt like it was my time to experience the wrath of God and go to the place where I knew I belonged–*hell*.

I stared at this veiled image of God Himself for at least three seconds. Pulverized by shame, my insides were shredded like never before. I turned away in disgrace and remained like this for what felt like an eternity but was maybe 30 seconds. Eventually, the load of this presence lifted, and peace slowly began to flood the room.

As I walked to the couch, I did not dare to look to see if He was still there. In a pretzel-legged position and my eyes closed, I suddenly felt a sensation on my kneecaps and a GIANT right hand resting on my head. The definition of every finger was so real as the hand covered every square inch of my head. I felt like a newborn baby with my father's hand on my head. The terror completely vanished, and peace continued to pour in beyond measure. Full of mercy, love, and grace, the hand resting on my head made me completely forget that moments ago, I thought I was going to a place I thought did not exist.

Unable to comprehend this rollercoaster ride, I eventually opened my eyes as everything faded away. This peaceful bliss remained with me the rest of the night, but as I stood up in disbelief, I tried to find a way to prove to someone what had just happened. I was unsuccessful, but I did not care because this was the best moment in my entire life.

No more than an hour later, I was ready to go to bed as I thought this insane encounter was over. As I lay in bed, I suddenly felt these sensations as if I was the subject of a fireman's carry. I never left the bed, but it felt as if an angel grabbed me under my arms, and another angel lifted my legs to transport me to an unknown place. These sensations were similar but slightly different from the hand on my head, but they were so defined that I could feel the pressure points as if someone was truly in physical contact with me.

Puzzled for weeks, I tried to understand the sensation on my knees when the hand rested on my head. It finally occurred to me that if I were seated in a pretzel-legged position and someone was standing over me with their hand on my head, their legs would have contacted my knees. Upon this realization, I was convinced no one could explain what had happened to me.

Unfortunately, the next day I made a mistake before I left the house. I sat next to my mom as she rested before her workday began and told her with a rather meek tone, "Mom, I think I saw God last night." This mistake eventually earned me two extended stays at the Veterans Affairs psychiatric hospital. As if my life had not already hit rock bottom, the next phase of my life went even lower.

Before we move on, I need to make two points. First, I was praying to God and never realized what I was doing. The self-improvement list - yeah, that was praying to God unbeknownst to me. Second, I should remind you I occasionally smoked marijuana during this time. My tolerance was pretty high, but I find it ironic the marijuana I used during all of this was called "Hell's Angels."

Not Going to Church

The diagnosis of ADHD and Adderall changed many things in my life. The list of improvements is long, but my mother stood firm that nothing was wrong with me. She was against this treatment and promised if I misbehaved with the medication, she would do anything to bring me down. When I told her I saw God, the flames of hysteria engulfed her.

Soon after, my mom freaked out. I was on the phone with a mental health doctor as I drove to Wal-Mart that afternoon. They asked me to stop by to talk about what had happened. In my belief that this was a simple misunderstanding, I agreed to meet because I had just been through the most incredible experience in my life. Surely the doctors would understand what happened to me, I thought.

I sat face-to-face with this female doctor, and she told me I experienced a psychotic episode, or what a doctor calls a break from reality. I instantly knew this would be an uphill battle. I snapped back and asked her to define reality because what I went through was real. I was familiar with mind-altering substances, and this experience had zero similarities.

After much debate, she asked if I would check myself into the locked mental health unit for further evaluation. I declined and went on with my day, baffled as to why anyone would think I went off the deep end.

I then headed to Wal-Mart since I did not make it there earlier. Less than a mile away, my peripheral vision faded black, and I fell into this trance-like state. I quickly knew I had experienced something like this before.

In high school, a friend and I decided to race into a set of woods that has a hairpin turn for an entrance. In the 1990 Corvette my mom bought for me, we raced towards this corner rated for 15 MPH. I entered the corner as my friend slammed on his brakes, but the moment I realized 85 MPH was too fast, I was in deep trouble. My peripheral vision faded black, and the car drifted off the road in slow motion. Within inches of swapping paint with an oak tree, I escaped without knowing how I avoided naming the tree.

When this visual experience reappeared, I was intrigued as to what was about to happen. So, I decided to play along. It is difficult to explain because I believe you can only understand this if it happens to you, but I was being led somewhere. It went like this - when I arrived at an intersection, I waited. If I got a ping in an ear, I went in that direction. If I did not hear a ping, I went straight.

I had absolutely no idea where I was headed, and this January evening was eerie, to say the least. The snowy sky was dark, with undertones of purple and orange mixed in as if Picasso was in charge that night. Slightly afraid of the now slippery roads, I somehow remembered the Bible verse that speaks about walking through the valley of the shadow of death and fearing no evil.

I continued to follow this crazy ear music and was eager to discover where I was going. Then, in picturesque fashion, I saw this gigantic cross that lit up the night sky and penetrated my heart. I immediately started to cry as I discovered the purpose of this journey. I was being led to CHURCH!

With the recent thoughts of not wanting to go to church, I drove right past the church on purpose. I told this thing that led me to turn us around if that is where I should go. Well, it did. However, the ringing had stopped as this deep-seated longing to enter this church surfaced.

As I pulled into the parking lot, there were cars there for a Wednesday night gathering. Rather than going inside, I settled for a personal ceremony before the cross to spare myself the embarrassment once again. I told Jesus He got me as I accepted Him right then and there.

On my way home, this longing to enter the church bubbled over. Before I knew it, I wiped the tears from my eyes and opened the front door. Nobody at this Bible study said a word as I tried to act normal. They handed me the worksheet and continued.

The next thing they read from the study guide caused a waterfall of tears to break free. "Do you feel like life is a tug of war, and you are the rope?" My past relationship ended because I felt as if I met extreme resistance while I tried to accomplish what I set out to complete. I was pulled in every direction and fell to the floor in utter defeat on the day I left the relationship. I gave up on trying to be the person she wanted me to be.

With awkward looks as my tears interrupted the Bible study, I began to describe what had happened over the past 48 hours. I expected to be met as a crazy person, but the opposite happened. Everyone was amazed at what I told them and soon began to praise God. Once again, I could not believe it. Less than three hours ago, I was told by an "expert" that I required mental evaluation, but now I was told how God worked a miracle. The powerful flood of emotions settled as I knew I had found the place I was supposed to be.

The church was, in fact, for me!

The Battle Begins

Although I had this rock-solid conviction that I was 100% okay, I was frustrated because nobody believed me aside from these churchgoers. In hindsight, I do not blame anyone who concluded I was going through a psychotic episode, but it was an epic battle between two conflicting domains of thought.

After noticing the benefits medication had on my life, I realized I would run out and need another prescription. I continued to seek treatment from the Madison VA mental health team and simultaneously tried to convince these "experts" that I did not experience a psychotic episode. I tried hard to explain everything that happened, but it seemed like I was talking to a brick wall.

The doctors stood firm. They would not continue this medication unless I admitted myself into the locked psychiatric unit for further observation. After much hesitation, I agreed because I was afraid to go through another exam and face the crippling anxiety.

My first of two trips to the psych ward was, in a weird way, a great experience. I made a couple of new friends and discovered that whatever I had experienced was truly a unique situation. My first real activity was an interrogation by a panel of doctors. The lead doctor, who was a Muslim, continued to ask me these silly questions as if she literally thought I had journeyed into another dimension.

They asked their questions with this fake sincerity as if they were the superior holders of all knowledge and truth. The doctors either did not make an effort or simply did not understand my responses, so I became irritated at their line of questioning. I do not recall many of the questions, but this one question made me realize these doctors were completely blind to what happened to me.

"Did you receive any special powers?"

Thankfully, I was unaware of prophecy, the power of correctly interpreted dreams and visions, and the true healing power of God during this interrogation. I have experienced all of these "special powers" since, but this moment was certainly not the time to divulge this type of information. The false labels would have been super-glued, and I doubt I would have made it out of there.

I took their tests and challenged every label they tried to stick on me as I spent two days and three nights with them. I was open and honest about everything because I wanted the truth. I even admitted to misusing the medication! However, with a simple line of rebuttal questioning, none of the doctors could explain their diagnoses where I could understand them. I eventually felt like a dartboard as they threw everything they could at me.

I had a major fallout with my mom after she fed me to the wolves, so I left the hospital and headed to my dad's house. My frustration remained as I explained everything to my dad. Without a resolution and barred from the continuation of the medication, I was determined to understand the situation and get to the bottom of it. With a freshly packed bag and Valentine's Day flowers for the wonderful nurses, I knocked on the door of the locked psych ward unit, ready to go back in. I wanted help, and I wanted answers.

Unexpectedly, I was turned away, and my jaw hit the floor when they told me ADHD is not treated in their unit. The day prior, I was given a list of personality disorders and labeled bipolar, but when I returned to seek further help, I was told they do not treat ADHD at this clinic.

I could *not* believe it.

Since I completely abandoned the way of finding drugs on the street, I turned back to my primary mental health doctor for more help. Before Adderall entered the picture, this doctor and I played the Pharmaceutical Roulette game and went through a few different medications to relieve ADHD symptoms, but nothing worked. They were now convinced I lied about the symptoms but decided to try another path of medication. The medication that worked for me was no longer an option, so we tried one last medication.

By now, the clock was ticking before I was too far behind to catch up or even complete my classes. It was a do-or-die. The last medication of this game was, by far, the weirdest one for me. I am not certain if it was the medication or my situation, but I started to have strange thoughts of hurting myself. Sure, my life had ups and downs, but I had never considered hurting myself. When these thoughts started to enter my mind, I was legitimately concerned.

I had one last phone call with the doctors at the Madison VA facility. I do not remember the exact words they used, but they told me that if the current medication was not working for me, I was on my own.

Frustrated, angry, and disappointed, all the hope I had was now gone. I sent a nasty text message to my mother, "If you find me hanging in a tree, I will see you in hell." I then wrote an ambiguous note to my father that said I was going away and not sure when I will be back. I got into my car and hit the road. With my cell phone turned off and outraged at the world, I drove off with no idea where I was going. There was soon a state-wide manhunt (Green Alert) and another psych ward visit right around the corner.

Because mental health is a complicated subject, I do understand the human brain is complex, and we humans have little understanding of it. I understand why doctors have to play guessing games, but in my situation, this guessing game was uncalled for. Did Adderall help? Yes.

The Battle Begins

Did I misuse the medication? Yes, I did. Did I confess my transgressions and try to find solutions? Yes. Did I have the support system in place to ensure abuse would not happen again? Yes. But for whatever reason - being afraid of losing their job, medical license, or whatever the case may be-these doctors were not going to treat me with this medication anymore.

All Hope Lost

This encounter with God instantly changed me. Minus a few situations of choice words for my mother and doctors, my foul mouth was completely cleansed. The trash music I listened to changed as well. However, this joyride to nowhere brought the old me back to center stage. As I drove and cursed the world, I listened to the old music that I despised. I even cursed God too. I promise you–it was very ugly.

About an hour and a half into this ride, I passed a church, and the sign read, "Eternity, think about it." These words did not jump at me as previous experiences had, but this sign spoke deep into my being. It was a challenge. Believe it or not, it made me angrier toward God. I yelled back, "Oh yeah. Do this again. I dare you!"

Challenge accepted.

The very next church I passed had another sign that related to eternity as well. It felt as if God spoke to me and directly challenged me to think about what the heck I was doing. When I realized God spoke to me, all of my attitudes did a 180 towards Him. This heavy burden was lifted when I discovered God was actually listening to me.

I was still upset at the world, but my anger toward God completely disappeared. I ended up near our old family cabin near Tipler, WI, as I drifted away in a conversation with God. I decided I was not going back to the world that night and took my 2004 Honda Accord off-roading where we used to deer hunt years ago. In case you were wondering, yes, the Honda got stuck, and I spent the night in the woods.

The next afternoon, I flagged down a good Samaritan who pulled my car out of this mud pit. My heart sank as I spotted two Florence County Sheriff Deputies waiting near the entrance. I knew exactly why they were there.

"Do you know how many people are looking for you?"

Never did it occur to me that there was a Green Alert sent out, and news stations across Wisconsin published information about my road trip. When I powered up my phone at the police station and saw the inflow of phone calls and messages, I could not help but think about what I had done. I did not exactly try to create a scene, but on the other hand, I wanted to create a scene because nobody tried to listen to me. So, is this really what it takes to be heard?

Please try to understand this–I was twenty-nine years old and one semester away from accomplishing my dream of graduating from UW-Madison's business school. My GPA was about 3.7, and I cared deeply about my grades. I also wanted to get on with my life. I gave it everything I had, but I was unable to make it through my classes.

In hindsight, I could have tried harder to push through and graduate regardless of the final grades. But at this time, I could not do college without medication as I was gripped with testing anxiety and fear.

In the back of the police car and on my way to the Tomah VA facility for my second stay in the psych ward, I was partially relieved I had finally gotten someone's attention. The next day, I discussed what had happened with the lead doctor. He was unlike any doctor before. It did not take long to notice I had finally found a doctor who could explain things at a deeper level.

This doctor and I went back to the beginning, where I had the encounter with God. Everything did not make perfect sense, but much of what he said sounded plausible. He explained that snorting Adderall can cause psychosis, and he had at least some reasonable explanation for some other things we discussed. A counselor even told me about his psychotic experience of him shooting rabbits from his toilet seat. This made me realize people do have some off-the-wall experiences.

Before I slept that night, I deeply reflected on everything. I played back the experience with God over and over again. I wanted to know the truth, no matter how painful it was to hear. As I questioned everything that had happened, I cried myself to sleep, thinking this incredible experience was just fake.

As I woke up in a room designed to prevent creative suicide, I rose, planted myself, and said, "No, what I experienced was real." And that was it - no one could tell me otherwise. I was now determined to understand the disconnect between what I experienced and what these doctors believed happened to me. One of us was right, and I was not about to settle for medical book theory. If they knew the truth, then they were required to clearly explain everything to me. An expert should be able to explain even the most complicated subjects to a five-year-old. Over the next 10 days, I set out to find the truth, the whole truth, and nothing but the truth.

I completed several different questionnaires which tried to label me as this or label me as that. With each new label, I sincerely asked questions to gain understanding. With every line of questioning, the doctors eventually ran out of explanations as to why this label fits me. Every dead end led to another round of questionnaires. This cycle repeated a few times, and eventually, I determined these doctors tried whatever they could to see if anything would stick. I cannot speak of every situation, but in my case, it was clear they did not know what they were doing. Ironically, two of my fellow roommates even told me, "Jordon, you are not crazy. These doctors are not listening to you."

The lead doctor did gain my intellectual respect, but he eventually lost it while he preached the importance of mindfulness. He told me all about mindfulness while his face was buried in conversation on his phone. As his patient who went through a serious situation, his obvious display of hypocrisy was the final nail in the coffin.

However, I still wanted to know the truth. I was sincere with my questions, but my questions were also legitimate. In fact, one of the psychologists graduated from a Bible school, and we had the chance to get deep into my experiences. So round and round we went. He never admitted this, but I could see he knew what I went through was different. He even tried to drop hints to the lead doctor, but this doctor blew a gasket when he realized someone had tried to undermine his mental evaluation authority.

My stay here ended with me on yet another medication that did not work in the long run. Oddly enough, I thoroughly enjoyed my time here as well. It was super interesting to hear about others and what they were going through. We had group therapy sessions and learned some great tips on certain topics.

Poor mental health is a real thing, as I learned while in this unit. Unfortunately, what I discovered is the methods used to diagnose are questionable at best. One thing that caught me by surprise in the psych ward was that a majority of the patients had some biblical foundation. The other patients and I often talked about God, Jesus, and the Church. But between doctor and patient, these conversations were rarely discussed. If they were discussed, they were never taken seriously. Maybe it is time to take this seriously.

As I looked ahead at how I was going to rebuild my life, I left the Tomah VA facility eager to get started.

Do you need help?

I am sure mental health professionals help many people every day. I believe that someone reading this should feel it is good to seek and receive help even if others tell of unsuccessful treatment and results. I'm not a medical professional, and my story shares my perception of events. Please seek help until someone listens & takes action for emotional, mental, and physical health concerns.

Faith

Now faith is the assurance (title deed, confirmation) of things hoped for (divinely guaranteed), and the evidence of things not seen [the conviction of their reality–faith comprehends as fact what cannot be experienced by the physical senses]. ² For by this [kind of] faith the [a]men of old gained [divine] approval.

Hebrews 11:1-2

The battle was certainly not over after I left the VA facility, but things progressively improved from there. Progress seemed slow at times, but at other times it was quite apparent. Developing a relationship with a God who is invisible but ever-present has been a challenge. I can assure you; however, it is not boring. In fact, it is quite an adventurous journey.

I'd like to share a few stories that center around the faith to help illustrate how, little by little, God has helped me grow my faith.

When I talk about God and how He speaks to me, I need to clarify a few things. I believe God has His own way of talking to us as individuals, so the way He speaks to me might be different from how He speaks to others.

The process of discerning when God speaks can be described like this: trial and error. I am wrong more times than I am right, but over time I get better at hearing and seeing His communications. To keep it simple, I guess the best way to put it is when God speaks to you, you just know it is Him.

God's Faithfulness & Tithing

After my second and last trip to the psych ward, I was broke. I had enough money to last about six weeks, so I applied for jobs like crazy. I sent out at least 25 resumes as I looked for something to do before I knocked out my last semester of college. I never struggled to find a job my entire life until now. I often bounced between different jobs to pick up new skills for my toolbox, and whenever I wanted to pick up a new skill, I quickly found the right job. Out of all the resumes I sent out, I received just one automated response.

That was it. And I was devastated.

When I started this walk of faith, I began to give away 10% of all income, known as a tithe. This is something God asks of us as followers of Christ, so I committed to this with all I had. I continued to tithe during this jobless period, and frankly, I had no business tithing. I was almost out of money, and I needed every dollar I could save. But I did it anyway.

With about two weeks left before I was completely cashed out, I was in church on a Wednesday evening when God spoke to me. He said I was going back to work for the company I had recently left. I laughed, of course, as I considered that ship had sailed. I told Him to have them call me if this is true. This same evening, my old company called me and asked if I could do some work for them.

I was stunned.

Not only was God faithful to me in this moment, but it got even better. About a month after I started working again, I got a $10 per hour raise! In six weeks, I went from being completely drained of money to having the highest salary in my life. This salary was beyond my expectations for a single guy with a semester in college remaining. The company even paid me a salary while I finished my last semester of college. Only God could have drawn this up on the drawing board.

Paying Off Debts

I gave up my shot glass invention as I thought about how I could not support binge drinking and carry the name of Jesus too. I have nothing against responsible drinking, but I could no longer promote binge drinking. So, I closed up shop and took on a huge pile of debt. It was a burden and more than I could handle. I even turned down an offer of $12,000 to purchase my patent. As of this writing, I am still working on this debt, but there was one situation where I had a personal loan of about $10,000 that had a high payment and high-interest rate.

God spoke to me before my final semester and said, "this personal loan will be paid off before I graduate." Once again, I laughed and thought about how crazy this sounded. Sure, I was getting a nice salary, but to pay off $10,000 of debt in less than five months seemed crazy. To make matters worse, I was required to pay UW Madison over $3,000 to return since I dropped out the previous semester. I had taken advantage of the financial aid, and it needed to be repaid.

I flipped out when this debt was added to the already massive pile. I yelled at God and asked Him how in the world are we going to pay off this debt now. I briefly mocked Him and questioned whether it was Him or my selfish desires that spoke. Believe me, it was not pretty.

Sure enough, God came through. Not only was this $3,000 paid off (thankfully borrowed and returned from a good friend), but the $10,000 loan was paid off by March. I could not believe it when I had the money to pay off this loan six weeks early. It was truly incredible.

Healing Miracles

This story falls close to my heart for many reasons. As I browsed through Facebook one day, a high school classmate who struggled with drug addiction asked for help to get to a rehab facility in Arizona. I ignored this at first, but it bugged me for a few days. So, I got in my car, gave his parents money to help cover some expenses, and left him his first Bible. I gave him my testimony of snorting Adderall, how God completely set me free and went on my way. Never did I expect to hear from him again.

His rehab trip to this sober living facility was a complete disaster. I am not here to pass judgment, but eventually, I invited him to stay with me. Imagine a young man, beaten down by the guilt and shame caused by drug addiction without any hope for healing. He was lost, and nobody was able to help him.

God asked me to help him, specifically saying, "No matter the cost." For weeks, he joined me in my daily routine of waking up early and reading the Bible. I did my best to explain things to him, but more importantly, I tried my best to show him the love God has for him. I can assure you the process was painful for both of us.

He fractured his neck in a car accident three years prior. He could not work out as he wanted to, in fact, doing pushups was out of the question because the pain was so bad. Then one day, as we were driving, I noticed this warm and loving presence fill the car. I have no idea what gold tastes like, but I could taste this gold that permeated inside the car. I have never experienced anything like this before or even since.

At this moment, I knew God was with us. Bursting with love and joy, I looked at him and said, "Hey, dude, I bet your neck does not hurt anymore." While he touched his neck and tried to feel the pain, he was also shining with this brilliance as if someone had come to life. Then he rolled his head and tested every which way that would cause the pain to flare up. His face was cemented in my memory when he looked at me and said, dude! My neck pain is gone."

I cannot explain what happened, but the healing experience was real. He tried everything to cause the pain to come back, but it never returned. Every time I saw him after this moment, he was on the ground doing pushups. It was a surreal experience I will never forget.

Another healing miracle happened weeks later with the same person. During a car ride, I noticed my friend in what looked like torment. He was twitching and moaning as if the pain was shooting throughout his body. To be honest, I was clueless. Either way, I knew something was wrong, so I prayed with the authority of Jesus over him.

"Out in the name of Jesus"–and he instantly went back to normal.

I suppose I expected something magical to happen when I prayed; however, that was definitely not the case. No taste of gold, no feeling of special power inside me, or even a heavenly beam of light in sight. When we made eye contact, I said, Dude, I cannot believe that worked!"

"Yeah, me too," he said.

It crushes me to say this, but shame and addiction still have a hold on his life. I said I would never give up on him, but until he is ready to get back on the horse and fight with me, I will be on the sidelines waiting for him. Bro, if you ever read this, I am here for you. God loves you. Jesus loves you. You are forgiven. *Never forget this!*

On a quick side note, I have to admit that I had a false belief during this time. I thought that I needed to be perfect or holy for God to work miracles through me. However, these events occurred while I continued to struggle with pornography and nicotine addictions. I know it sounds crazy, but it is the truth!

Other Witnessed Miracles

My typical Saturday consisted of fellowship at a believer's home, and one evening, they invited an Evangelical Healing Minister over. Considering this was my first experience with a healing minister, I was not sure what to expect, and I was not disappointed. This man, full of passion, preached a short sermon and then went to each of us in the room and prayed for a specific request. There are two instances I will never forget.

The first person asked this minister to pray for his pinky finger. The elderly man had a pinky finger that would not go straight. It was permanently curled into his palm and caused a lot of discomfort. The minister went up to this guy, prayed in the name of Jesus, and BAM. This pinky shot straight out as if the spring-loaded tension was released. My eyes popped open with amazement as I witnessed the smile on the old man's face.

The second case was another man who had "normal" congestion. On the same side, his ear and nostril were plugged, and he could not get them clear. The minister walked up to him and prayed in the name of Jesus, but nothing happened. The minister never skipped a beat and prayed two more times. Then BAM, the congestion was gone. The man who was prayed for sat there and continued for five minutes in amazement. He could not believe his congestion was gone.

I have many more stories, both great and seemingly insignificant. But here is the thing, nothing is too big or too small for Jesus to take care of. I promise it is not easy and often feels like doubt, but God has used many life situations to build my faith in Him.

I like to call Him the God of midnight-thirty because He seems to show up when I believe it is too late. However, His timing has always been near perfect. He comes through every time, and each time He is faithful, it helps grow my faith more and more.

Hope

Hope: to trust in, wait for, look for, or desire something or someone; or to expect something beneficial in the future.

Nobody is guaranteed an easy life; in fact, many influencers of today's society faced intense trials and tribulations during their lifetime. Who are we to be the exception? Although we are expected to face many unforeseen challenges, that never means we should give up hope.

God Chose Someone for Me

I believed my past relationship before my face-to-face with God was the person whom I would spend the rest of my life with. I mean, I thought we were perfect together. She was smart, hardworking, and had a wonderful family who fully accepted me. Unfortunately, I was afraid to be fully transparent with her regarding my life struggles. I was afraid to tell her about my nicotine usage, pornography addiction, and how I threw Adderall up my nose almost daily. I take full responsibility for catering to this fear which ultimately destroyed me.

But God had different plans, and I am thankful for how He has worked in my life. Shortly after my extended stay in the mental hospital, God spoke to me and said the next date I go on would be with my wife. I made a promise to Him that I would not mess around with women or go on dates until I was sure about the commitment. The next year and a half dragged on as I was impatient and always searching for the person God had for me. Every time I thought a particular girl was the one, God snapped back and never helped me make the connection.

During this time, I used this Christian dating app, but it required a paid subscription. After a few attempts, I eventually gave up. Occasionally, this app would give me free access for a few days, so I would check it out but often be disappointed.

For months, I would drive past this billboard on my daily commute that said, "Better CAN Happen." For some reason, the sign spoke deeply into my heart. I knew someone was to come, but I had no idea about the timing.

Eventually, God spoke to me and said the next season of my life was called "Fulfillment." I did not understand what He meant, but five months later, I received a message from the dating app. In full-blown patience mode, I opened the app without knowing what would come next.

When I saw the profile of the person who winked at me, my jaw hit the floor. She was stunningly beautiful, educated, and loved God. My first thought was, why in the world would this person be talking to me?

I noticed she lived in Brazil, and without skipping a beat, God reminded me of my desire for a foreign wife. I fell in love with the idea of a foreign wife during my time in Germany. The experiences of different cultures and speaking a new language is what I have always been interested in. It blew my mind to think God was the one who reminded me of my own desires.

I responded to this wink without much hope, to be honest. I have been through this dating game before. But when she wrote back, we instantly hit it off. With the scars from my past relationship, I made it a point to tell her all of my nasty traits to avoid being trapped in that dreadful fear again.

I unloaded all of it as I thought, if this is really from God, then she would accept me as I am. If she decided I had too much baggage, I was okay with this as I had learned to be content where I was. I told her about my porn struggles, nicotine addiction, my past drug use, and everything else that made me feel insecure. For some reason, this made her more attracted to me. She was fed up with everyone trying to promote themselves regardless of the truth. She never met anyone who would come out and say the dirty stuff, especially within the first conversation. Anyway, it worked!

We spent time together online for the first four months and got to know each other on a deep and personal level. We read marriage books and discussed life with God. She told me about prophecies she received when she was a teenager, and we discovered they were eerily similar to what I received within the last year.

A month before we met, a stranger told her God would give her the husband she was looking for. I never believed God had someone just for me, but after I learned about these prophecies, we were both 100% convinced. I then traveled to Brazil to meet her and her family. I traveled to more than 16 countries, and I can confidently say Brazil was my favorite experience of them all! Rio de Janeiro is the most beautiful city I have been to, and the food in Brazil blows every country out of the water!

Adventures to NYC

My wife and I married when she came to visit me in Wisconsin. We had no serious intentions of getting married so quickly, but we knew we needed to either make a firm commitment or part ways.

Around this time, there was an opportunity to do some consulting for a new kosher food production startup in Brooklyn, New York. We discussed this opportunity and decided to just go for it. We had some incredible moments and met some amazing people, but this trip came with many more challenges than we anticipated.

All these challenges taught me a few key life lessons. The first is just because God has something or someone for you; it does not guarantee an easy path. The American and Brazilian cultures clash, and they clash quite hard. I lost count of how many times I had to eat my own words, humble myself, and ask my wife for forgiveness because I was impatient, inconsiderate, or just being a big jerk. I mean this deeply–she has a very forgiving spirit!

The second thing I learned was that God was always looking out for my desires, but they do not always come when we demand them to come. Although I was thankful and enjoyed the job I previously wrote about, I craved something more. I wanted to do something, anything more than what this company was willing to do. I created different visions and found potential revenue streams with the main focus of improving customer service. When the leadership balked at these ideas, and I was more than open to feedback, I knew my time there was short. Prayers were up, and God answered the call.

The final thing I would like to share, although not an exhaustive list, is when God calls you to do something, He will provide the means and the ways to do it. The day I accepted the opportunity in NYC, I calculated the cost of moving and settling in. Without any relocation assistance, the total out-of-pocket cost was about $8,000. This amount was so far out of reach in our current situation, but in the next 30 days or so, we had all the money necessary to move.

The same happened on our way back to Wisconsin after completing this opportunity. We decided to head back to Wisconsin since it would be the best place to raise our unborn baby girl. We left on April 1st, but the month prior, we spent everything we had as we helped my old classmate check into another drug rehab program. I could not even buy my wife a birthday gift because we had no money to spend.

It was that bad.

Brazilian culture is big on gifts. I grew up in a large family, so gifting was never a priority. We would all be poor if we sent out gifts for the four parents, eight siblings, and nine and counting nieces and nephews. But this moment crushed me. I had some choice words for God when I realized we had no money. I shouted Bible verses back at Him and recited the promises He made known in His book. Honestly, I was angry, ashamed, and felt betrayed. This knocked me off my feet for over a week.

But somehow, and in some way, God provided. When I got over my temper tantrum, and as I lay in bed, God clearly said He would show up in church the next day. Sure enough, someone handed me $100 with the exact Bible verse I kept shouting back to God. I hate to admit this, but God often makes me eat my own words and take my medicine. His patience with me has been absolutely incredible, I might add.

To be honest, we had an overabundance, and to this day, it still puzzles me how it all happened. I am good with math and numbers, and I have tried to backtrack to figure out how we had so much money. Either I am overconfident in my abilities, or a true miracle took place because I cannot explain step-by-step how all this money came to us.

For I Know the Plans I Have for You

God works in mysterious ways, but sometimes, He speaks plainly about things to come. It is too early to make a public announcement or any such declaration, but I know what God has planned for me because He showed me in a very supernatural way. I do not know how this will happen or the timing, but I know He has plans and a future for my family and me.

Never give up hope. There will be peaks and valleys, but I encourage you to learn every step of the way. God is faithful and will never leave you nor forsake you as long as you follow Him. God isn't afraid to hear your deepest thoughts, fears, and insecurities. Yes, even when you are upset with Him. He already knows you are mad, so why not just come out and say it? He knows you better than you know you, and never forget this!

'For I know the plans and thoughts that I have for you,' says the Lord, 'plans for peace and well-being and not for disaster, to give you a future and a hope. *12* Then you will call on Me and you will come and pray to Me, and I will hear [your voice] and I will listen to you. *13* Then [with a deep longing] you will seek Me and require Me [as a vital necessity] and [you will] find Me when you search for Me with all your heart. *14* I will be found by you,' says the Lord, 'and I will restore your fortunes and I will [free you and] gather you from all the nations and from all the places where I have driven you,' says the Lord, 'and I will bring you back to the place from where I sent you into exile.'

Jeremiah 29:11-14

Love

Love endures with patience and serenity, love is kind and thoughtful, and is not jealous or envious; love does not brag and is not proud or arrogant. ⁵ It is not rude; it is not self-seeking, it is not provoked [nor overly sensitive and easily angered]; it does not take into account a wrong endured. ⁶ It does not rejoice at injustice, but rejoices with the truth [when right and truth prevail]. ⁷ Love bears all things [regardless of what comes], believes all things [looking for the best in each one], hopes all things [remaining steadfast during difficult times], endures all things [without weakening]. ⁸ Love never fails [it never fades nor ends]. But as for prophecies, they will pass away; as for tongues, they will cease; as for the gift of special knowledge, it will pass away.

1 Corinthians 13:4-8

In the past, I thought my concept of love was correct. If I felt a certain way, regardless of my thoughts or actions, I was a loving person. Upon learning more about Jesus, I realized just how wrong I was.

I do not aim to preach my concepts of love but to demonstrate how the love of God has affected my life. God sent Jesus, who in human flesh was fully God and fully human simultaneously. But Jesus, to save us and bring us back into a relationship with God, decided to take the punishment for everyone's sins. I have often thought about taking a bullet for someone, and I hope if the situation ever presented itself, I would have the courage to do so.

But Jesus, who could have said screw it as He tried to help the people who were nailing Him to a piece of wood, dared to die for even the worst of humanity. Jesus even asked God to forgive the people who were actively killing Him. Who would ever do something like this, and why? This demonstration illustrates just how difficult it is to fully comprehend the love of God toward each and every person.

Pornography

One moment that really changed me occurred a year after my encounter. I attended church often and read the Bible numerous times. I understood what the Bible was saying, but I noticed some disconnect between what the Bible said and how the church portrayed God.

Although my pornography addiction was much improved, I continued to fall into the temptations and was not strong enough to withhold my behaviors. This brought me great shame, and I struggled to believe Jesus could not help me because I continued to act this way.

One day in the shower, I put my foot down on these thoughts of shame and said to myself, "No, you said that you love me no matter what." Knowing this behavior was unacceptable; I decided to believe God still loved me. It was settled, and I never looked back.

The pornography did not end right then and there, but what did end was the extreme shame that fell upon me after I caved into these temptations. I knew I was not perfect and often struggled, but this turning point allowed me to discuss my challenges openly. It took great courage to discuss pornography with others, but it became quite easy over time. Many people have thanked me for this courage because it has helped them talk about their struggles. I hope my story empowers you to have the courage to talk about your struggles too!

Judgment of Others

Yet another change happened inside of me after I read the Bible numerous times and developed this relationship with God. The way I looked at others changed. I did not believe I was a judgmental person in the past, but I discovered I am a judgmental person. But now, I have a much greater understanding and patience that looks at people from a different perspective. Jesus is full of truth, grace, mercy, love, and everything else we desire as humans. If I fully believe Jesus could love me as I am, how dare I look towards others with a judgment of any kind? It is a daily battle in this arena, but it is a battle worth fighting.

When I decided to help my high school classmate with his drug addiction, I looked to him as Jesus saw me. I did my best to have compassion, understanding, and patience with him. In a similar jam with Adderall, I thought I would be a great person to help him realize how much God loved him and break his addiction for good. I also think I changed more than he did in the process!

Although things did not work out, I would never hesitate to do it all over again. When I tried my best to show him the expansiveness of love God had for him, I could see the change in his eyes. It was incredible, almost addicting, to see someone so broken come back to life. In hindsight, there are some things I would change about our time together, but I am a human too. I am not God and cannot make anyone believe and maintain the revelation and a relationship with God. Each of us needs to take this journey alone.

My Mother

Forgiving my mom for all the things she had done was one of the most difficult things to do. She hysterically sold me out to doctors after the most incredible experience of my life. Was I misbehaving? Yes. Did I deserve some type of correction? Of course, I did! But at every corner, it seemed as if all she wanted to do was take me down.

It was obvious I was holding onto some other pain as well. I also brought up my true feelings on how she abandoned us, brainwashed us, and was not the best example that a mother could be. I held onto this unforgiveness for a long time, and it was evident.

I hate being a hypocrite. I am still capable of being what I despise, but the biggest reason why I was able to forgive my mother was because of Jesus. Jesus had forgiven me of all the things I had done. I was set free from snorting Adderall. I was set completely free from pornography. I was set free from negative thought patterns. I was set free from many things which caused great pain and hindered me from becoming the best version of myself. So how in the world could I not forgive my mother?

This forgiveness did not happen overnight. It was a lengthy and ugly process. However, I can say this from the bottom of my heart–Mom, I forgive you.

The World Today

I believe many people would agree with me - we all need to show more love toward one another. I am guilty like everyone else, but I do know the solution to evil is not evil but love. Furthermore, we know the truth will set us free, but the truth spoken without love is empty and destructive. Love is what will help solve our problems, and it starts in the church.

If I shut up the heavens so that no rain falls, or if I command locusts to devour the land, or if I send pestilence and plague among My people, [14] and My people, who are called by My Name, humble themselves, and pray and seek (crave, require as a necessity) My face and turn from their wicked ways, then I will hear [them] from heaven, and forgive their sin and heal their land.

2 Chronicles 7:13-14

Unconditional Love of God

Remember the shame I carried from my pornography behaviors? To this very day, I am so very thankful I believed in what the Bible says about me. Jesus took upon Himself the sins of this world. Jesus took upon Himself my sins. And Jesus took upon Himself the sins of you, too!

There is absolutely NOTHING that can separate us from the *UNCONDITIONAL* love of God. Nothing means N-O-T-H-I-N-G! Let me be even clearer and provide examples to combat those "what about this" thoughts inside your head:

- Abortion

- Homosexual behavior

- Transgender ideology

- Sexual misconduct of any kind

- Drug addiction

- Abuse of power

- Verbal abuse

- Physical abuse

- Judgment of others

- Lying, cheating, and stealing

- Unloving behavior

- Fill in the blank

I am guilty of many of these

Are you still struggling? Let us keep going. Did your drug addiction cause you to do things that continue to stir your stomach? Were you the aggressor in a horrible situation, and you cannot find it in yourself to forgive yourself? Does that hole in your heart continue to throb and bring you to your knees from killing your own baby? If this is you, check out these two stories from the Bible about King David and the Apostle Paul.

King David was known as the man after God's own heart. You might be familiar with the David and Goliath story, but did you know David used his influence to commit adultery with a woman who he accidentally knocked up? And to avoid the political fallout, King David tried to get her husband to sleep with her to make it seem as if this child was theirs. However, his plan failed, so he sent him to the front lines of the battlefield. The man was killed.

God then sent a prophet to King David to call him out. David recognized his appalling actions and repented, but God still provided a punishment and killed the baby born out of adultery. Oddly enough, when the dust settled, King David and God continued and remained in a close relationship. He knew of God's incredible ability to forgive even the worst of all behaviors!

Furthermore, the Apostle Paul may have been even worse than King

David. Paul, a religious zealot, relentlessly hunted and killed Jesus' followers. Paul thought he was doing God a favor as he hunted these people night and day. Jesus supernaturally appeared to him and then transformed Paul to become one of the greatest spiritual authorities in history!

So now consider what you have done. Can you honestly say you are worse than King David or the Apostle Paul? If you want to continue to hide in shame, I can list a dozen more examples. I will answer the question for you. No, you cannot say you are worse than any Biblical example. And you can easily discover this truth by reading your Bible.

Break free from your prison of shame today! Shame is not from God, and everything has been forgiven and forgotten. Period. End of story.

Redemption Inc.

God is holy, and part of being holy is sticking to your word. When God told Adam and Eve not to eat the fruit from the tree of good and evil, it was irrevocable. It could never be undone. After Adam and Eve did the unthinkable, God was required to bring about the separation between

Him and man and boot them from this paradise on earth.

Thankfully, God is in the redemption and restoration business too. He had a backup plan, and the backup plan was Jesus. He said, "I cannot renege on my word, so I will send Jesus to take the punishment and sentence Him to an extremely painful death." The only condition we have to meet is to believe in our hearts that God sent Jesus and that He took the punishment we deserve. It is that simple to get back to this paradise on earth and to inherit eternal life in heaven. This plan allowed God to maintain His integrity and keep His word, and at the same time, rescue His creation from the awful curses He proclaimed.

I have found that believing in your heart simply means believing God loves you no matter the circumstances.

No matter what you said.

No matter how you feel.

No matter what you have done.

It does not matter!

There is nothing unforgivable except blasphemy of the Holy Spirit, but I will save the meaning of this for you to discover another time. This may come as a shock, but God can forgive while society remains at your throat. Chew on that for a while.

It is also important to understand we cannot use God's promise of love to then do whatever we want to do. This is an abuse of God's love. It is deadly to think we can continue in unrighteous behaviors while believing that God approves. However, we can trust God's love when we understand our unrighteous behaviors are wrong. The difference is the state of mind during our agonizing transformation.

Known by God

What is it like to know and be known by Him? How does it feel to be 100% exposed to the Creator, who knows absolutely everything? Surprisingly, it is incredibly freeing and is by far the most adventurous quest you will ever experience. It is both awe-inspiring and challenging at the same time. You will experience and witness miracles, tested beyond your capabilities, and laugh and cry often when you discover God is real and very active in your life. I also guarantee you have never met anyone with a better sense of humor than God!

If you have ever witnessed a poor representation of God by religious zealots, carry resentment towards Him for any reason, or need to see to believe, I hope to inspire you to forget everything and discover Him on your own. I wish I could provide a formula that would help you discover

God, but to my knowledge, Wikipedia does not have one. I believe the reason is His creation is so complex and intelligently designed that one size does not fit all.

However, I do know step one is repentance. My advice is to be as sincere as possible and take an inventory of yourself and your actions. Take a hard look and get into the muck of the things you have done and what has happened in your life. Be honest about everything, and do not try to justify anything. Call it like it is! This is where Jesus hangs out, so if He wants to meet you, this is where you start. Repentance is an incredible gift, but I do not expect this to make sense for a while.

After repentance, pray and seek God. God made a promise that if you seek Him, you will find Him. Try to find Him working in your daily life. It is hard for me to believe in coincidences anymore, so if something comes across as a coincidence when you search for God, it is likely Him at work.

During this phase, also read through and do the things Jesus preached about in His sermon on the mount. Trust me; it is impossible to be perfect in all of those things in the sermon but give it your best effort.

See what happens.

The relationship between you and God is strained badly. God is very emotional, so if He does not respond right away, just be patient. Try your very best to be sincere about wanting to meet Him. You cannot fool God because He already knows, remember?

And lastly, if you are sincere to the best of your ability, just give it time. He will show up when you least expect it. This has happened to many people I know, and my wife is a perfect example of this. She chased after God but gave up when He did not show Himself. He arrived shortly thereafter.

God the Heavenly Father

You never met a perfect Father, but that is who God is. Believe it or not, God does not sit on His throne in heaven and send down wrath and lightning bolts for sport. He does, however, correct as a loving Father should. As a perfect Father, He can provide all the things (character traits, provisions, correction, etc.) you would need to accomplish the purpose and mission you were created for.

Without a doubt in my mind, we all have a purpose and mission, and it is His ultimate desire for you to accomplish these things! He is willing and more than capable of turning your life around. He did it to me, and I know He would do it for you too. I urge you to discover and listen to the voice inside that has confirmed you indeed have a purpose and a mission, even if you do not know exactly what it is.

What is the role of a Heavenly Father?

Surprisingly, it is not far off compared to what we look for in a human father. Basically, it is the same relationship dynamic, except you are dealing with a Father who knows everything and is unable to be fooled. You can lie to and manipulate your earthly father, but your Heavenly Father is impossible to manipulate. I have tried, and it does not work, trust me!

As a Heavenly Father who desires to help you accomplish your purpose, He does this by conforming you to become like Jesus in character. God will do whatever it takes to first turn you into a representation of Jesus, and then from there, your life will move accordingly. The process could and likely will be ugly. It could get really ugly, but it is totally worth it. My process was ugly and still is at times, but I am so thankful I never quit. I hope you and I have the courage and strength to keep going and never give up!

The Challenge

There is something I do not understand in this world. Why do we accept someone else's version of the truth before we conduct our own investigation on the matter? At the very least, we know there are often three sides to every story, so why are we so quick to accept someone's version of God and not investigate the matter on our own?

The Bible and the truth are available to everyone, so why do we depend on someone else to tell us how it is? By trial and error and extreme humility, we should all go out and do our own research on God. It is impossible to mess this up because God's level of patience is mind-blowing.

In fact, I challenge you to determine if what I say about God is even true or not. I say this cautiously, but I urge you to learn and develop your own relationship with God before you blindly follow the pastors and church leaders of today. They can be helpful and a resource, from which I have benefitted, but the risk of running into a fake leader is quite high. Sadly, false leaders are everywhere. These false leaders are often out of touch and blind, but more importantly, they rob themselves and others of the true wealth of life with God.

And please, run away as fast as you can if anyone thinks a college degree gives them the authority to lead you to God. This could not be further from the truth! Who knows Michael Jordan better and would be able to explain to others who he is? Would it be the basketball historian who can rattle off every single stat and smash through trivia questions for breakfast? Or would it be Michael Jordan's family members, whether it be his father, mother, or child? The relationship matters much more than a piece of paper or even time in service in a dead church.

I will leave you with this. God does not want to do a transformation TO you; He wants to do it WITH you! God does not need anything from us but desires our attention, affection, and love. He wants to know us intimately, and this relationship cannot be earned by trying hard enough or attending a college degree program. This relationship is a gift made possible through the unfathomable, incomprehensible, and all-encompassing love proved by the sacrifice made by Jesus Christ.

Afterword

The events I wrote about are 100% true and accurate, but I wrote the start of the first chapter from memory and sparse notes. I have a detailed journal about the few days leading up to the run-in with authority, but the dates beforehand are simplified and condensed to tell the story concisely.

Also, I left out many stories that did not fit into my story as constructed. For example, I once heard this audible voice whisper, "Jesus. Devil. Devil. Devil." This repeated three times and occurred between the time I started attending church and my first psych ward visit. I had intense visions of Jesus on a cross, other surreal sensations with angels, and inspiring moments when God used license plates to speak to me.

Finally, I have one last confession. The battle to draft this story was intense and almost never happened. For nearly two years, I confronted the following thoughts and fears:

- No one would want to hear my story.

- I do not have the talent to write a book.

- What will my family think about my struggles, especially the pornography stuff? YUCK!

- What will the people whom I lied to think about me?

- Will anyone even buy this book that I worked so hard to write?

- You name it; I battled it!

After numerous attempts that ended in failure, I completed the first draft within two weeks. The words just poured onto the pages, and this was a miracle within itself.

One would think after the first draft was completed miraculously, the rest would have been a cakewalk. Nope, I continued to struggle throughout the process. The event that pushed me over the edge of fear and doubt was when my good friend, Michael, provided encouragement after he read the rough draft. After this encouragement, I knew I had a story that must be shared.

My story is to be continued…

Acknowledgments

Thank you to:

Vanessa Helena

Michael Hernke

Andre Gemeinder

Bruno Gemeinder

Joel Dunbar

Lori Schultz

Each of you helped encourage me to complete this project in one way or another.

www.ingramcontent.com/pod-product-compliance
Lightning Source LLC
LaVergne TN
LVHW051219070526
838200LV00064B/4968